All the Best Songs of Praise & Worship 2

More Contemporary Favorites

Compiled by
Ken Bible, George Baldwin, and Marty Parks

Music edited by
Marty Parks

LILLENAS
PUBLISHING COMPANY

1

Blessed Be Your Name*

Nehemiah 9:5

M. R. and B. R.

MATT REDMAN
and BETH REDMAN

1. Bless - ed be Your name in the land that is plen -
2. Bless - ed be Your name when the sun's shin - ing down

- ti - ful; Where the streams of a - bun - dance flow, bless-
- on me; When the world's all as it should be, bless-

ed be Your name; Bless - ed be
ed be Your name; Bless - ed be

Your name when I'm found in the des - ert place, When I
Your name on the road marked with suf - fer - ing; Tho' there's

Jesus, Draw Me Close

James 4:8

2

RICK FOUNDS

3

What the Lord Has Done in Me*

Joel 3:10

1. Let the weak say I am strong. Let the poor say I am rich. Let the blind say I can see. It's what the Lord has done in me.
2. Into the river I will wade, There my sins are washed away. From the heaven's mercy stream. Of the Savior's love for me.
3. I will rise from waters deep Into the saving arms of God; I will sing salvation's song— "Jesus Christ has set me free!"

CHORUS

Hosanna, hosanna to the Lamb that was slain. Ho-

san - na, ho - san - na, Je - sus died and rose a - gain.

Forever*

Psalm 136

4

CHRIS TOMLIN

C. T. ♩ = ca. 120

1. Give thanks to the Lord____ our God and____ King;
might - y hand____ and out - stretched arm;____ His
ris - ing to____ the set - ting____ sun____

love en - dures____ for - ev - er.
And by the grace of God____ we will

For He is good,____ He is a -
For the life_____ that's

bove all____ things;____
been re - born;____ His love en - dures____ for - ev - er.
car - ry on;____

Sing

5 You're Worthy of My Praise

Matthew 22:37-38

D. R.

♩ = ca. 110

DAVID RUIS

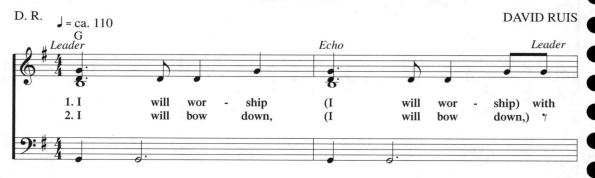

1. I will wor - ship (I will wor - ship) with
2. I will bow down, (I will bow down,)

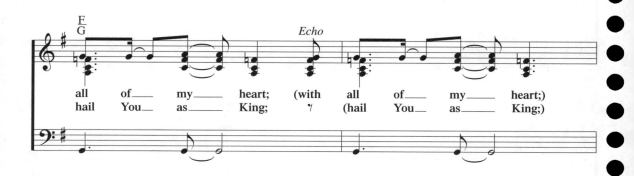

all of my heart; (with all of my heart;)
hail You as King; (hail You as King;)

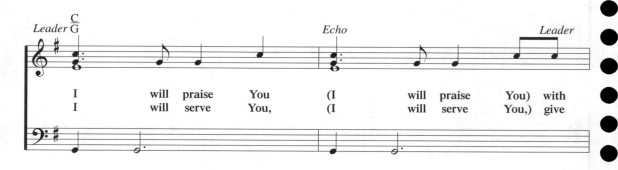

I will praise You (I will praise You) with
I will serve You, (I will serve You,) give

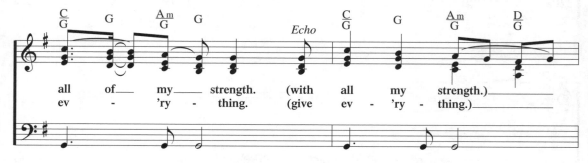

all of my strength. (with all my strength.)
ev - 'ry - thing. (give ev - 'ry - thing.)

all my praise.___ You a-lone___ I long to wor - ship,

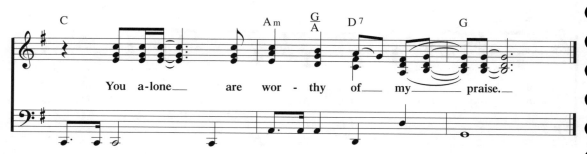

You a-lone___ are wor - thy of___ my___ praise.___

6

He Knows My Name*

Psalm 139:1-16

T. W.   ♩ = ca. 80

TOMMY WALKER

Unison

1. I have___ a Mak - er,___
2. I have___ a Fa - ther,___

He formed___ my heart;___   Be - fore___ e - ven time___
He calls___ me His own.___   He'll nev - er leave___

7

Jesus, What a Savior*

Titus 3:3-7

S. W.

SHANNON WEXELBERG

1. You are my strength when all my strength has end -
2. You are my rock when I need a place of ref -
3. You see the world with eyes full of com - pas -

- ed. You are my hope when
- uge, A hand reach - ing out when I
- sion. You feel the hurt of the

all my hope is gone. You are my
stum - ble and I fall. You are my
lost and wound - ed soul. Lit - tle chil - dren can

joy when my world is full of sor - row. You're the
all in ev - 'ry time and sea - son. You are
know that Your gen - tle arms will hold them. You can

You Are My Hiding Place

Psalm 32:7

M. L. ♩ = ca. 84

MICHAEL LEDNER

9 Open Our Eyes

Ephesians 1:18

BOB CULL

Here I Am to Worship*

10

Psalm 95:6

T. H.

TIM HUGHES

1. Light of the world, You stepped down in-to dark - ness,
2. King of all days, O so high - ly ex-alt - ed,

O - pened my eyes, let me see
Glo - rious in heav - en a - bove,

Beau - ty that made this heart a - dore You,
Hum - bly You came to the earth You cre - a - ted,

Hope of a life spent with You.
All for love's sake be - came poor.

my sin _____ up-on _____ that cross.

So here I am to _____ Here I am to wor-ship.

11   How Deep the Father's Love for Us*

1 John 4:10

STUART TOWNEND

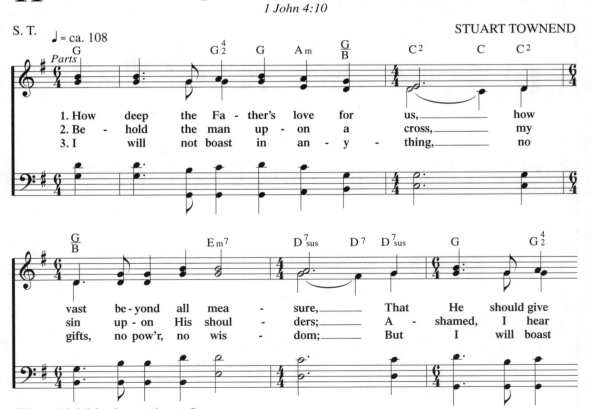

1. How deep the Fa-ther's love for us,_____ how
2. Be-hold the man up-on a cross,_____ my
3. I will not boast in an - y - thing,_____ no

vast be-yond all mea - sure,_____ That He should give
sin up-on His shoul - ders;_____ A - shamed, I hear
gifts, no pow'r, no wis - dom;_____ But I will boast

12

Beautiful One*

Psalm 18:1

T. H.

TIM HUGHES

♩ = ca. 120

1. Won - der - ful, so won - der - ful is Your un - fail - ing love,
2. Pow - er - ful, so pow - er - ful, Your glo - ry fills the skies,

Your cross has spo - ken mer - cy o - ver me.
Your might - y works dis - played for all to see.

No eye has seen, no ear has heard, no heart could ful - ly know How
The beau - ty of Your maj - es - ty a - wakes my heart to sing: How

- tured my heart__ with this__ love   'Cause noth - ing on earth__ is as beau-

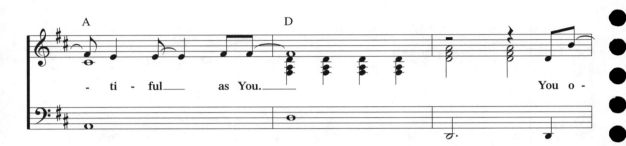

- ti - ful__   as You.__   You o -

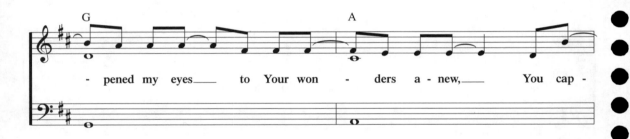

- pened my eyes__   to Your won - ders a - new,__   You cap -

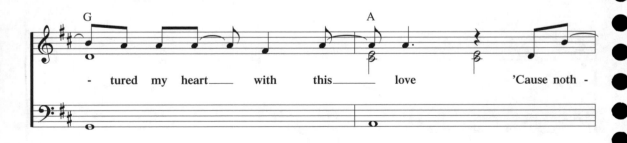

- tured my heart__ with   this__   love   'Cause noth -

- ing on earth__ is as beau - ti - ful__ as   You.__

13 Let It Rise

Isaiah 60:1

H. D.

HOLLAND DAVIS

Let the glo - ry of__ the Lord__ rise a - mong__ us, Let the

glo - ry of__ the Lord__ rise a - mong__ us. Let the

prais - es of__ the Lord__ rise a - mong__ us, let it rise.__

__ Let the

songs of__ the Lord__ rise a - mong__ us, Let the

14
Be the Centre
John 14:6

MICHAEL FRYE

15 Ancient Words*

2 Timothy 3:14-17

L. D.

LYNN DESHAZO

♩ = ca. 72

1. Ho - ly___ words, long pre - served, For our walk___
2. Ho - ly___ words of our faith Hand - ed down___

___ in this world;___ They re - sound with God's own
___ to this age;___ Came to___ us thro' sac - ri -

heart, O let the an - cient words im - part.
fice, O heed the faith - ful words of Christ.

Words of___ life, words of hope, Give us strength,
An - cient__ words, long pre - served, For our walk___

16 Indescribable*

Psalm 104

LAURA STORY and JESSE REEVES

LAURA STORY

Verse lyrics:

1. From the high-est of heights to the depths of the sea, Cre-a-tion's re-veal-ing Your maj-es-ty.

2. Who has told ev-'ry light-ning bolt where it should go Or seen heav-en-ly store-hous-es la-den with snow?

From the col-ors of fall to the fra-grance of

Who i-mag-ined the sun and gives source to its

Jesus, Your Name

Acts 4:12

17

C. C. and M. C.

CLAIRE CLONINGER
and MORRIS CHAPMAN

1. Je - sus, Your name is pow - er; Je - sus, Your name is might. Je - sus, Your name will break ev - 'ry strong - hold; Je - sus, Your name is life.
2. Je - sus, Your name is heal - ing; Je - sus, Your name gives sight. Je - sus, Your name will free ev - 'ry cap - tive; Je - sus, Your name is life.
3. Je - sus, Your name is ho - ly; Je - sus, Your name brings light. Je - sus, Your name a - bove ev - 'ry oth - er; Je - sus, Your name is life.

18 Breathe*

John 20:22

MARIE BARNETT

M. B. ♩ = ca. 62

This is the air I breathe, this is the air I breathe, Your ho - ly pres - ence liv - ing in me. This is my dai - ly bread, this is my dai - ly bread, Your ver - y Word spo - ken to me.

19 You Are Holy (Prince of Peace)

Psalm 99:1-3

M. I. and T. R.

MARK IMBODEN and
TAMMI RHOTON

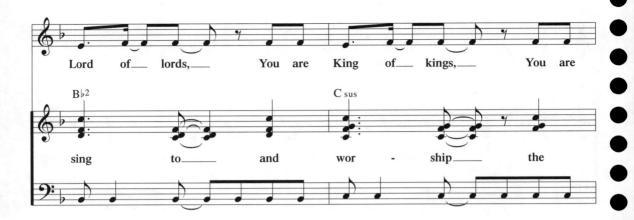

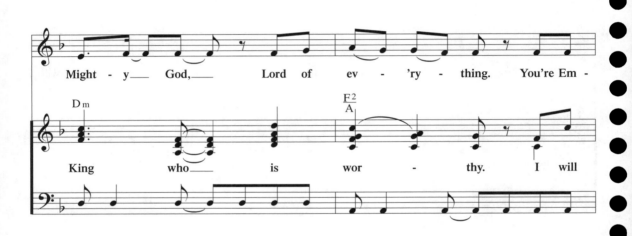

Prince of_ peace_ who_ is_ the_ Lamb. You're the

bow down_ be - fore_ Him. I will

liv - ing_ God,_ You're my sav - ing_ grace._ You will

sing to_ and wor - ship_ the

reign for - ev - er, You are An - cient_ of Days. You are

King who_ is wor - thy. I will

Worthy Is the Lamb*

Revelation 5:11-14

D. Z.

DARLENE ZSCHECH

*This song is included on the companion recording.

21
Lord, Have Mercy
Psalm 123:3

S. M. ♩ = ca. 56 STEVE MERKEL

Lyrics:

1. Je-sus, I've for-got-ten the words that You have spo-ken;
Prom-is-es that burned with-in my heart have now grown dim; With a
doubt-ing heart I fol-low the paths of earth-ly wis-dom;
For-give me for my un-be-lief, re-new the fire a-gain.

CHORUS
Lord, have mer-cy; Christ, have mer-cy;

Rise Up and Praise Him*

Psalm 96:1-4, 11

P. B. and G. S.

PAUL BALOCHE
and GARY SADLER

23

How Great Is Our God*

Psalm 104:1-2

C. T., E. C. and J. R.

CHRIS TOMLIN, ED CASH
and JESSE REEVES

1. The splen - dor of___ the King___
2. Age to age,___ He stands___ and

clothed in maj - es - ty,___ Let all the earth___ re - joice,
time is in___ His hands,___ Be - gin - ning and___ the End,

let all the earth___ re - joice. He wraps___
Be - gin - ning and___ the End.___ The God -

Him - self___ in light___ and
head, three___ in one,___

*This song is included on the companion recording.

He Is Our Peace

24

Ephesians 2:14; 1 Peter 5:7

Adapted by K. G.

KANDELA GROVES

25 Famous One*

Psalm 145:3

C. T. and J. R.

CHRIS TOMLIN and JESSE REEVES

You____ are the Lord,____ the fa-mous One, fa-mous One;

Great____ is Your name in all____ the earth.____ The

heav - ens de - clare____ You're glo-ri-ous,____ glo-ri-ous;

Great____ is Your fame be-yond____ the earth.____

1. And for
2. The

26 I Can Only Imagine

1 John 3:1-2

B. M.

BART MILLARD

♩ = ca. 80 N.C.

Unison

1. I can on-ly i-mag-ine what it will be like when I walk by Your side. I can on-ly i-mag-ine what my eyes will see when Your face is be fore

27 Days of Elijah*

Deuteronomy 18:15-18; 1 Kings 17:1; Isaiah 40:3;
Ezekiel 37:1-14; 1 Thessalonians 4:16

R. M.

ROBIN MARK

1. These are the days of E - li - jah, de -
(2.) these are the days of E - ze - kiel, the

clar - ing the Word of the Lord. And
dry bones be - com - ing as flesh. And

these are the days of Your ser - vant, Mo - ses,
these are the days of Your ser - vant, Da - vid, re -

righ - teous - ness be - ing re - stored; And
build - ing a tem - ple of praise. And

*This song is included on the companion recording.

at the trum - pet call. So lift your

voice, it's the year of Ju - bi - lee,_____ and out of Zi - on's

Hill sal - va - tion comes.

2. And

comes.

28 Let My Words Be Few*

Psalm 18:1

M. R. and B. R.

MATT and BETH REDMAN

1. ⁷ You are God in heav - en,_____ and here____
2. The sim-plest of all love_____ songs,____ I want

*This song is included on the companion recording.

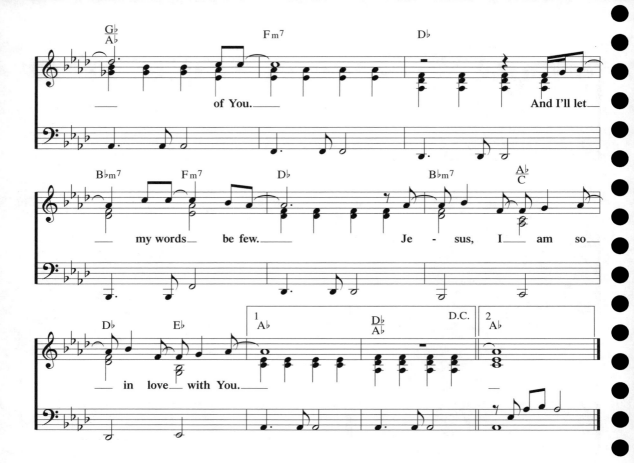

of You. ___ And I'll let ___ my words ___ be few. ___ Je - sus, I am so ___ in love ___ with You. ___

29   I Come to the Cross*

John 12:32

B. B. and B. S.

BILL BATSTONE
and BOB SOMMA

I come to the cross seek-ing mer - cy and grace; I come to the cross where You died in my ___ place. ___ Out of my

30

God of Wonders*

Psalm 77:14; Isaiah 6:3

M. B. and S. H.

MARC BYRD and
STEVE HINDALONG

The Father's Song

Zephaniah 3:17

31

M. R.

MATT REDMAN

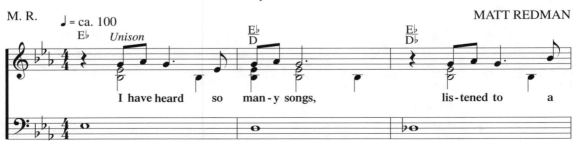

32 Offering*

Hebrews 13:15

P. B. ♩ = ca. 66

PAUL BALOCHE

The sun— can-not com-pare— to the glo-ry of— Your love;

There is— no shad-ow in— Your pres-ence;—

No mor - tal man would dare— to stand— be-fore— Your throne.

Be-fore— the Ho - ly One— of Heav-en;— It's

on - ly by— Your blood and it's on - ly thro'— Your mer - cy,

33 That's Why We Praise Him*

Acts 10:36-43; Philippians 2:5-11

T. W.

TOMMY WALKER

1. He came to live, live a per-fect life, He came to be the Liv-ing Word, our Light; He came to die so we'd be rec-on-ciled, He came to rise to show His pow'r and might. And

2. He came to live, live a-gain in us, He came to be our con-q'ring King and Friend; He came to heal and show the lost ones His love, He came to go pre-pare a place for us.

CHORUS
Parts

*This song is included on the companion recording.

34 Wonderful, Merciful Savior*

Revelation 5:11-14

D. R. and E. W.

♩ = ca. 120

DAWN RODGERS
and ERIC WYSE

1. Won - der - ful, mer - ci - ful Sav - ior, Pre - cious Re -
2. Coun - sel - or, Com - fort - er, Keep - er, Spir - it we
3. Al - might - y, in - fi - nite Fa - ther, Faith - ful - ly

deem - er and__ Friend;_____ Who would have tho't that a
long to em - brace;_____ You of - fer hope when our
lov - ing Your__ own._____ Here in our weak - ness You

35 The Power of Your Love*

Isaiah 40:31

G. B.

GEOFF BULLOCK

1. Lord, I come to You,_____ let my heart be_____
2. Lord, un - veil my eyes,_____ let me see You_____

_____ changed,_____ re - newed._____ ⁊ Flow - ing from the
_____ face_____ to face,_____ the know-ledge of Your

grace that I've found_____ in
love as You live_____ in

You. And Lord, I've come to know_____
me. ⁊ Lord, re - new my mind,_____

draw me to Your side. And as I wait I'll rise up like the ea - gle And I will soar with You, Your Spir - it leads me on in the pow'r of Your love.

36 Everything Within Me Worships You*

Matthew 22:37-38

S. S.

SUSAN SACCA

1. My heart, my soul, my mind, My
(2. With) ev - 'ry breath I take, As

37

We Will Dance*
Revelation 7:9-17

D. R.

DAVID RUIS

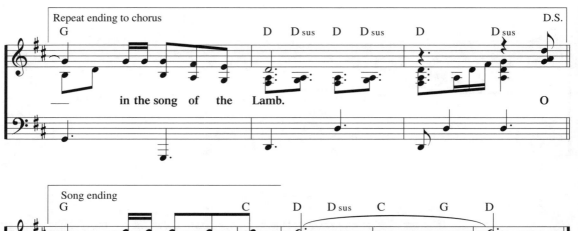

38 Sing for Joy*

Psalm 100:1-2; Jeremiah 33:3; James 4:8

LAMONT HIEBERT

L. H. ♩ = ca. 112

1. If we call___ to Him, He will an - swer us;
2. Draw___ near___ to Him, He is here___ with us;

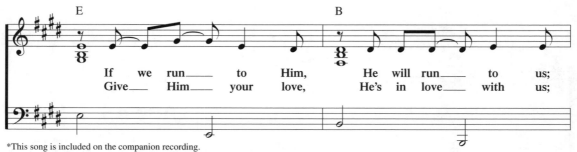

If we run___ to Him, He will run___ to us;
Give___ Him your love, He's in love___ with us;

39 Hallelujah (Your Love Is Amazing)*

Romans 8:35-39

B. D. and B. B.

BRIAN DOERKSEN and
BRENTON BROWN

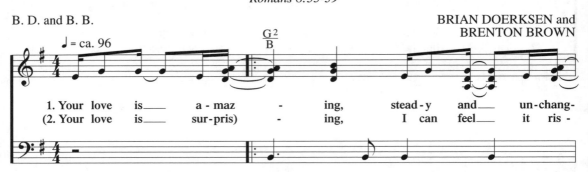

1. Your love is____ a - maz - ing, stead - y and___ un - chang-
(2. Your love is____ sur - pris) - ing, I can feel___ it ris -

- ing, Your love is____ a moun - tain, firm be - neath__ my feet;__
- ing, All the joy___that's grow - ing deep in - side__ of me;__

___ Your love is____ a mys - t'ry, how You gen - tly lift__
___ Ev - 'ry time__ I see___ you, all Your good - ness shines__

____ me When I am__ sur - round - ed, Your love car - ries me.
through, I can feel__ this God____ song, ris - ing up__ in me.

How You make me sing.

Seek Ye First

Matthew 6:33

40

KAREN LAFFERTY

K. L.

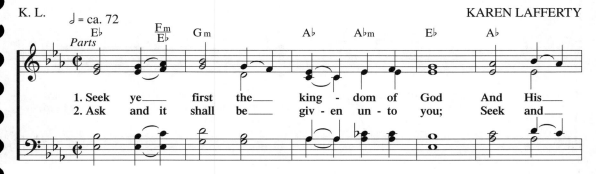

1. Seek ye first the king - dom of God And His
2. Ask and it shall be giv - en un - to you; Seek and

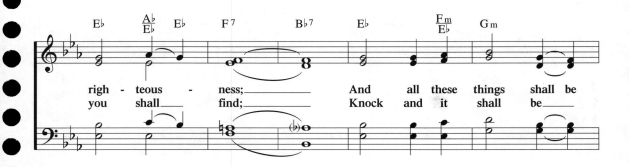

righ - teous - ness; And all these things shall be
you shall find; Knock and it shall be

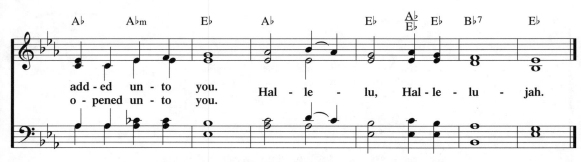

add - ed un - to you. Hal - le - lu, Hal - le - lu - jah.
o - pened un - to you.

41 Lord, Reign In Me*

Psalm 97:1; Matthew 6:9-10

B. B. ♩ = ca. 92

BRENTON BROWN

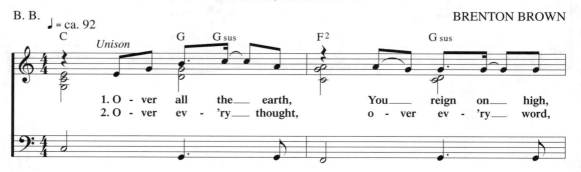

1. O - ver all the__ earth, You__ reign on__ high,
2. O - ver ev - 'ry__ thought, o - ver ev - 'ry__ word,

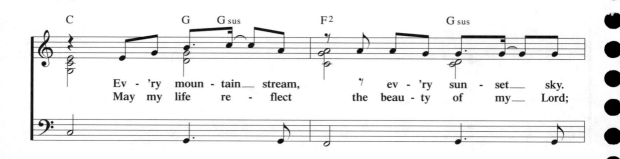

Ev - 'ry moun - tain__ stream, ev - 'ry sun - set__ sky.
May my life re - flect the beau - ty of my__ Lord;

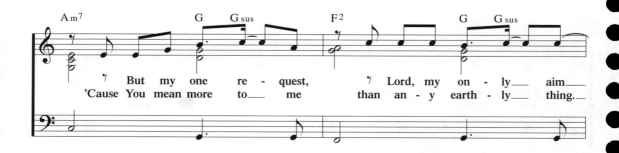

But my one re - quest, Lord, my on - ly__ aim__
'Cause You mean more to__ me than an - y earth - ly__ thing.__

CHORUS

Is that You'd reign in me a - gain. Lord, reign in__ me,
So won't You reign in me a - gain.

*This song is included on the companion recording.

So won't You reign in me a-gain. ___ Won't You reign in me a-gain. ___ Won't You reign in me a-gain.

42

In Christ Alone*

1 Corinthians 3:11

S. T. and K. G.

STUART TOWNEND
and KEITH GETTY

♩ = ca. 68

1. In Christ a - lone   my hope is found, _____ He is my
2. In Christ a - lone–   who took on flesh, _____ Full - ness of
3. There in the ground   His bod - y lay, _____ Light of the
4. No guilt in life,   no fear in death, _____ This is the

light, my strength, my song;   This cor - ner - stone, _____ this
God in help - less babe.   This gift of love _____ and
world by dark - ness slain;   Then burst - ing forth _____ in
pow'r of Christ in me;   From life's first cry _____ to

43 Grace Flows Down*

2 Corinthians 8:9

D. B., L. G. and R. P.

DAVID BELL, LOUIE GIGLIO
and ROD PADGETT

44

Who Can Satisfy My Soul

Psalm 73:25-26; Zechariah 13:1; John 7:37-38

D. J.

DENNIS JERNIGAN

1. Who can sat - is - fy _____ my _____ soul _____ like
2. Liv - ing Wa - ter, rain _____ down Your life like on

You? Who on earth _____ could com - fort me _____ and
me, Cleans - ing me, _____ re - fresh - ing me _____ with

love me like _____ You do? _____ Who could ev - er _____ be _____
life a - bun - dant - ly. _____ Riv - er, full _____ of _____ life, _____

more _____ faith - ful, true?
I'll go _____ where You lead,

Make Me a Servant

Matthew 20:25-27

45

K. W.

KELLY WILLARD

Make me a ser-vant, hum-ble and meek; Lord, let me

lift up those who are weak; And may the prayer of my

heart al-ways be: Make me a ser-vant, make me a

ser-vant, Make me a ser-vant to-day.

46 Holy Is the Lord

Isaiah 6:3; Nehemiah 8:10

C. T. and L. G.

CHRIS TOMLIN and
LOUIE GIGLIO

re-nown. It's ris - ing up all a-round; It's the an-them of the Lord's re-nown. And to-geth-er we sing. -ry. The earth is filled with His glo - ry.

47

Hallelujah! For the Lord God Almighty Reigns*

Revelation 19:6-7

M. P.

MARTY PARKS

Hal-le - lu - jah! For the Lord God Al-might-y reigns.

48 Did You Feel the Mountains Tremble?

Psalm 24:7; 114:3-7

M. S. ♩ = ca. 128   MARTIN SMITH

1. Did you feel the moun - tains trem - ble?____
2. Did you feel the peo - ple trem - ble?____
3. Do you feel the dark - ness trem - ble

Did you hear the o - ceans roar
Did you hear the sing - ers roar
When all the saints join in one song,

When the peo - ple rose to sing of____
When the lost be - gan to sing of____
And all the streams flow as one riv - er____

Je - sus Christ, the ris - en One?____
Je - sus Christ, the sav - ing One?____
To wash a - way our bro - ken - ness?____

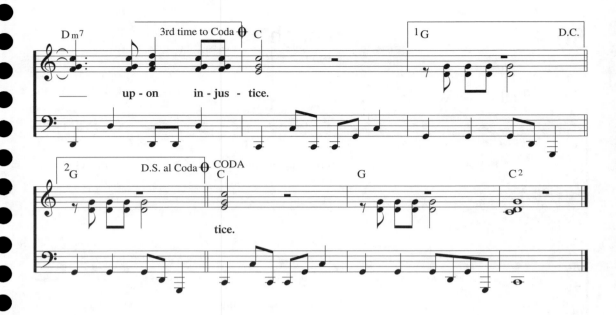

Fresh Anointing*

Acts 1:8

S. G. C.

SYDNEY G. COBLE

Lord, we need a fresh a-noint-ing; We can-not bor-row from yes-ter-day. Come and feed us, Ho-ly Spir-it, Teach us of Je-sus, His will, His way.

49

50 Enough

Colossians 2:9-10

C. T. and L. G.

♩ = ca. 78

CHRIS TOMLIN and
LOUIE GIGLIO

CHORUS *Unison*

All of you____ is more than e-nough____ for all of me,____

For____ ev-'ry thirst____ and ev-'ry need.

You____ sat-is-fy____ me with Your love,____

3rd time to Coda ⊕

And all I have__ in You is more than e-nough.__

1. You're my____ sup-ply,
2. You're my sac-ri-fice____

Yeah, You are more than e-nough for me.

More than all I know, more than all I can

say, You are more than e-nough. And all of You

CODA

You is more than e-nough.

51

He Is Able

2 Corinthians 9:8

R. N. and G. F.

RORY NOLAND and
GREG FERGUSON

♩ = ca. 72

Unison

He is a - ble, more than a - ble to ac-

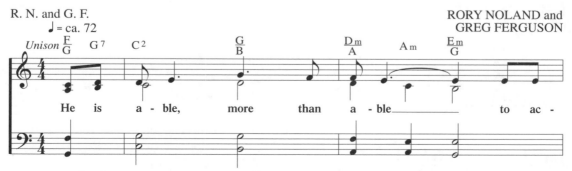

52

Be Thou My Vision*

Psalm 73:25

Traditional Irish Hymn

Traditional Irish Melody
Arranged by Marty Parks

1. Be Thou my___ Vi - sion, O Lord of my___ heart; Naught be all else to me, save that Thou___ art—
2. Be Thou my___ Wis - dom, and Thou my true___ Word; I ev - er with Thee and Thou with me,___ Lord;
3. Rich - es I___ heed not, nor man's emp - ty___ praise, Thou mine in - her - i - tance, now and al - ways;
4. High King of___ Heav - en, my vic - to - ry___ won, May I reach heav - en's joys, Bright Heav - en's___ Sun!

53 Lord, I Lift Your Name on High

Acts 10:36-43; Philippians 2:5-11

R. F. ♩ = ca. 110

RICK FOUNDS

Lord, I lift Your name on high;

Lord, I love to sing Your prais - es.

I'm so glad You're in my life;

I'm so glad You came to save us.

You came from heav - en to earth to show the

way; From the earth____ to the cross, my debt to

pay. From the cross____ to the grave, from the grave____ to the

sky; Lord, I lift Your name__ on high.____

As the Deer*

Psalm 42:1

54

M. J. N. ♩ = ca. 72

MARTIN J. NYSTROM

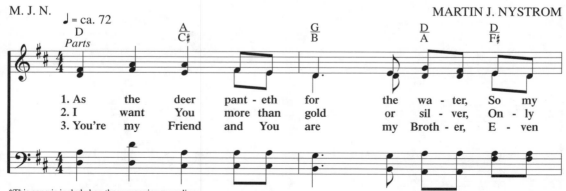

1. As the deer pant-eth for the wa-ter, So my
2. I want You more than gold or sil-ver, On-ly
3. You're my Friend and You are my Broth-er, E - ven

Come Just as You Are*

Ephesians 2:8

55

J. S.

JOSEPH SABOLICK

1. Come just as you are; Hear the Spir - it call.
2. Come just as you are; Hear the Spir - it call.

Come just as you are; Come and see, come, re - ceive;
Come just as you are; Come, re - ceive Christ, the King;

Come and live for - ev - er.
Come and live for - Life ev - er -

last - ing, and strength for to - day;— Taste the Liv - ing

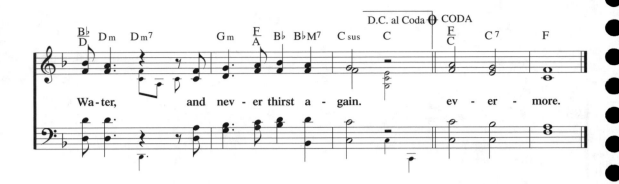

Water, and nev-er thirst a-gain. ev-er - more.

56 All Hail the Power of Jesus' Name*

Philippians 2:9-11

EDWARD PERRONET

OLIVER HOLDEN
Arranged by Marty Parks

hail the pow'r of Je-sus' name!__ Let an-gels__ pros-trate
cho-sen seed of Is-rael's race,__ Ye ran-somed__ from the
ev-'ry kin-dred, ev-'ry__ tribe__ On this ter - res-trial
that with yon-der sa-cred__ throng__ We at His__ feet may

fall. Bring forth the roy-al__ di - a - dem, And
fall, Hail Him who saves you__ by__ His grace, And
ball To Him all maj - es - ty__ as - cribe, And
fall! We'll join the ev-er - last-ing__ song And

57 Holy, Holy, Holy

Revelation 4:8

G. O.

GARY OLIVER

Holy, ho - ly, ho - ly, Holy, ho - ly, ho - ly, Ho - ly is the Lord God Al - might - y; Wor - thy to re - ceive glo - ry, Wor - thy to re - ceive hon - or, Wor - thy to re - ceive all our praise to - day. Praise Him,

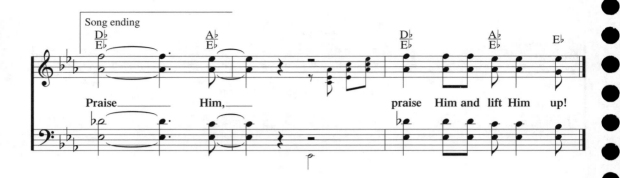

Praise_____ Him,_____ praise Him and lift Him up!

58

God of All*

Psalm 57:9-11

T. P.
♩ = ca. 86

TWILA PARIS

God of all,____ we come to praise__ You.____ We

lift Your name__ on high____ in all the earth.____

God of all,____ we come to praise__ You.____ We

*This song is included on the companion recording.

59 No Greater Love

John 15:13

TOMMY WALKER

T. W.

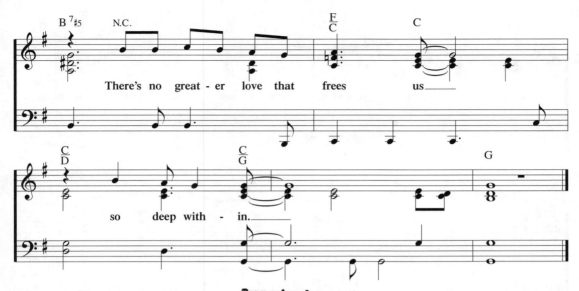

There's no great-er love that frees us
so deep with-in.

60 We Declare Your Majesty

Psalm 104:1

M. D. P.   ♩ = ca. 76   MALCOM DU PLESSIS

Unison

We de-clare Your maj-es-ty; We pro-
claim that Your name is ex-alt-ed! For You
reign mag-nif-i-cent-ly, rule vic-to-ri-ous-ly,

The Cross of Love*

John 12:32

61

CHRIS MACHEN

*This song is included on the companion recording.

62

(I Will Enter His Gates)
He Has Made Me Glad
Psalm 100:4

L. V. B.

LEONA VAN BRETHORST

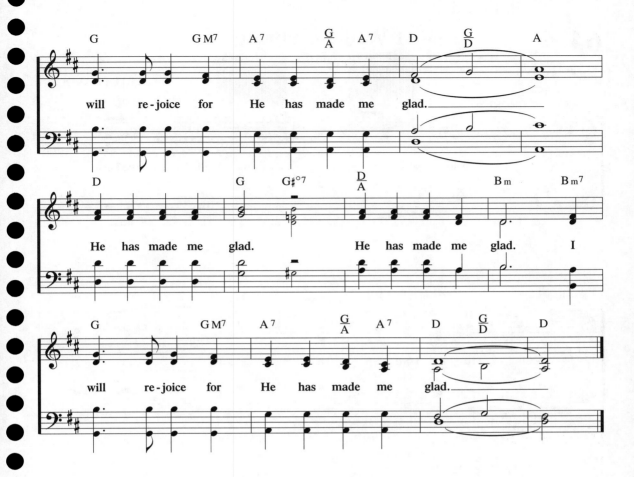

Thy Word

63

Psalm 119:105

Adapted by AMY GRANT

MICHAEL W. SMITH

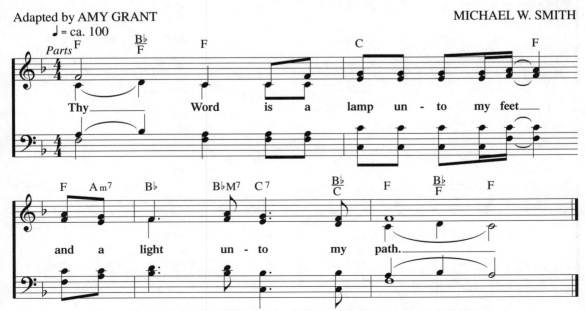

64 I Will Celebrate

Psalm 104:33

R. B.

RITA BALOCHE

65 We Will Worship the Lamb of Glory*

Revelation 5:11-14; 19:16

D. J.

DENNIS JERNIGAN

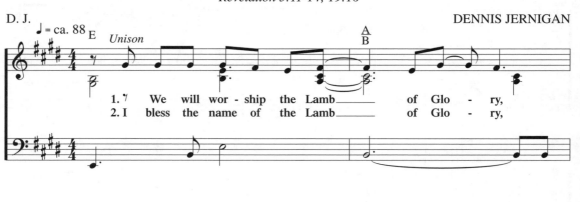

1. We will wor - ship the Lamb of Glo - ry,
2. I bless the name of the Lamb of Glo - ry,

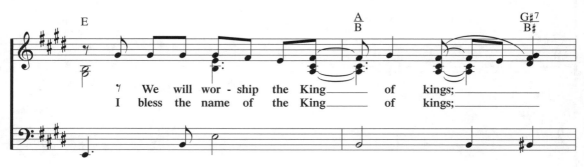

We will wor - ship the King of kings;
I bless the name of the King of kings;

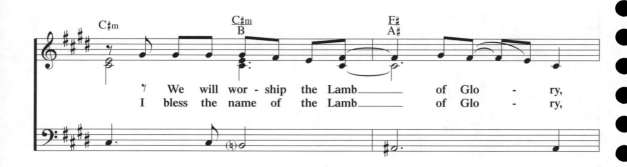

We will wor - ship the Lamb of Glo - ry,
I bless the name of the Lamb of Glo - ry,

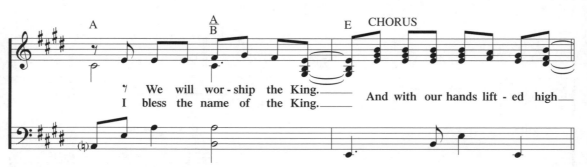

We will wor - ship the King.
I bless the name of the King.

And with our hands lift - ed high

*This song is included on the companion recording.

we will wor - ship and sing; And with our hands lift - ed high

we come be - fore You re - joic - ing. With our hands lift - ed high

to the sky, when the world won - ders why, We'll just tell

them we're lov - ing our King.

Hungry

66

(Falling on My Knees)

Psalm 42:1-2

KATHRYN SCOTT

1. Hun - gry, I___ come to You, for___ I know You sat - is -
2. Bro - ken, I___ run to You, for___ Your arms are o - pen

Cares Chorus

1 Peter 5:7

67

KELLY WILLARD

I cast all my cares up-on You. I lay all of my bur-dens down at Your feet. And an-y time that I don't know what to do, I will cast all my cares up-on You.

68 Humble Thyself in the Sight of the Lord

1 Peter 5:6

1 Peter 5:6

BOB HUDSON

Glorify Thy Name

John 12:28

69

D. A.

DONNA ADKINS

♩ = ca. 76

1. Fa - ther, we love You, we wor - ship and a - dore You;
2. Je - sus, we love You, we wor - ship and a - dore You;
3. Spir - it, we love You, we wor - ship and a - dore You;

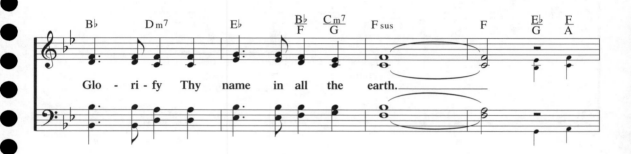

Glo - ri - fy Thy name in all the earth.___

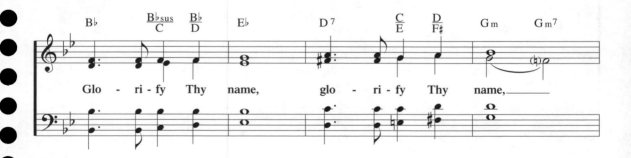

Glo - ri - fy Thy name, glo - ri - fy Thy name,___

Glo - ri - fy Thy name in all the earth.___

70 Come, Thou Fount of Every Blessing*

1 Samuel 17:12; James 1:17

ROBERT ROBINSON

Traditional American Melody;
John Wyeth's *Repository of
Sacred Music, Part Second*, 1813
Arranged by Marty Parks

1. Come, Thou Fount of ev-'ry bless-ing, Tune my heart to sing Thy grace. Streams of mer-cy, nev-er

(2. Here I) raise my Eb-e-ne-zer; Hith-er by Thy help I'm come. And I hope, by Thy good

(3. O to) grace how great a debt-or Dai-ly I'm con-strained to be! Let that grace, now like a

*This song is included on the companion recording.

on it,
Mount of Thy re - deem - ing love.

dan - ger,
In - ter - posed His pre - cious blood.

im - age,
In Thy pres - ence I shall

Repeat ending
love.
blood.

2. Here I
3. O to

Song ending
stand.

Be Still and Know

71

Exodus 15:26; Psalm 46:10; Psalm 56:4

Adapted

Unknown
Arranged by David McDonald

1. Be still_____ and know that I_____ am God.
2. I am_____ the Lord that heal - eth thee.
3. In Thee,_____ O Lord, I put_____ my trust.

Be still_____ and know that I_____ am God.
I am_____ the Lord that heal - eth thee.
In Thee,_____ O Lord, I put_____ my trust.

Be still_____ and know_____ that I am God.
I am_____ the Lord_____ that heal - eth thee.
In Thee,_____ O Lord,_____ I put my trust.

72 Kingdom Prayer*

Matthew 5:3-12

D. A.

DAN ADLER

Lyrics:

1. Lord, we're bro-ken, bro-ken-heart-ed, Tired of go-ing our own way. We've been proud and self-suf-fi-cient, But we're bro-ken here to-day. Lord, we need Your pow'r with-in us, For we have none of our own.

2. Lord, we're mourn-ing, mourn-ing chil-dren, Mourn-ing o-ver sins in-side. For they're al-ways right be-fore us, Much too great for us to hide. Lord, we need Your pow'r with-in us, For we have none of our own.

3. Lord, we hun-ger and we thirst for Right-teous-ness that's not our own; For we see our self-ish mo-tives, Come and take Your right-ful throne. Lord, we need Your pow'r with-in us, For we have none of our own.

73 Let the Rivers Flow*

Isaiah 35:6-7; Joel 3:18

SUSAN SUCCA

*This song is included on the companion recording.

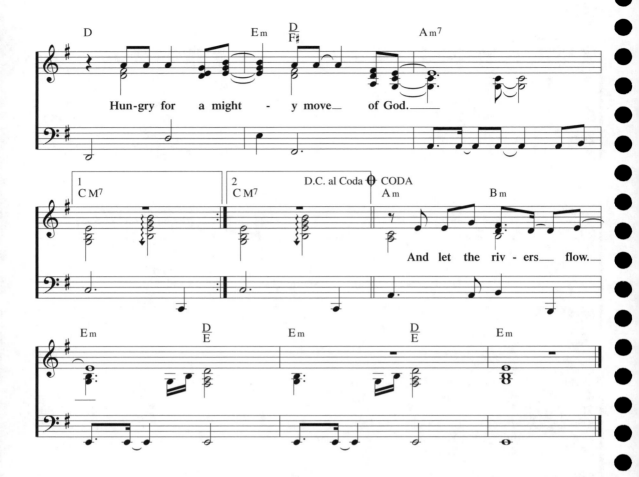

Hun-gry for a might - y move of God.

And let the riv - ers flow.

74 The Lord Is the Strength of My Life

Psalm 27:1-3

CHRIS MACHEN

The Lord is my Light, my sal -

va tion, Whom shall I fear? The

Come to the Child

John 1:14

75

76

I Long for Thee*

Psalm 42:1-2

C. and D. M.
♩ = ca. 64

CHRIS and DIANE MACHEN

1. As the deer pant-eth_ for wa-ter, So my soul_ long-eth af-ter Thee;_ My soul thirsts for You, the_ Liv-ing God, I long to be_ with You, with_ You.
2. Like the rose reach-es_ for sun-light, So I raise my hands_ to You, Lord;_ I will wor-ship You with my ver-y life, My heart de-sires on-ly You, on-ly_ You.

CHORUS I long_ for Thee,_ I long_

for Thee.__ Lord, how I__ long for Thee.____ I long__ for Thee,__ I long____ for Thee.__ How my soul long-eth af-ter Thee; How my soul long-eth af - ter Thee.

Better than Life

Psalm 63:3

C. C. R. and I. H.

♩= ca. 76

CINDY CRUSE-RATCLIFF
and ISRAEL HOUGHTON

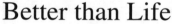

Unison   C(no 3)

1. Your love is ev - er - last - ing, it's an ev - er - last - ing__ love.__ Your
2. Fair - est of__ ten thou - sand, of ten thou - sand You__ are__ fair,__ And

78 'Tis So Sweet to Trust in Jesus*

Psalm 13:5; John 14:1

LOUISA M. R. STEAD

WILLIAM J. KIRKPATRICK
Arranged by Marty Parks

1. 'Tis so sweet to trust in Je - sus,
2. O how sweet to trust in Je - sus,
3. Yes, 'tis sweet to trust in Je - sus,
4. I'm so glad I learned to trust Thee,

Just to take Him at His___ Word, Just to rest up -
Just to trust His cleans - ing___ blood, Just in sim - ple
Just from sin and self to___ cease, Just from Je - sus
Pre - cious Je - sus, Sav - ior,___ Friend; And I know that

on His prom - ise, Just to know: "Thus saith the___
faith to plunge me 'Neath the heal - ing, cleans - ing___
sim - ply tak - ing Life and rest, and joy and___
Thou art with me, Wilt be with me to the___

*This song is included on the companion recording.

79

Have Your Way

Psalm 40:8

C. C. and D. M.

CLAIRE CLONINGER
and DON MOEN

Have Your way,_____ (Have__ Your__ way,)_____ have Your way;__

(have__ Your__ way.)_____ Ho - ly Spir - it, fill__ our hearts__

and have__ Your way._____ As we wait,__

(We wait on__ You,)_____ as we pray,__ (we pray to You.)

80 Fullness of Joy

Psalm 16:11

P. S.

PAULA STEFANOVICH

1. When I come in-to Your pres-ence, there is full - ness of joy,—
(2. When I) come in-to Your pres-ence, there is ev-er-last-ing love,—

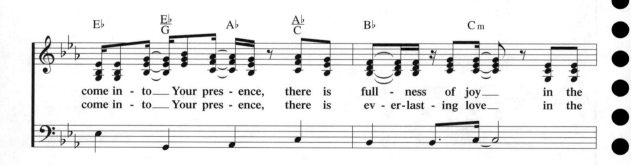

full - ness of joy,— full - ness of joy.— When I
ev-er-last - ing love,— ev-er-last - ing love.— When I

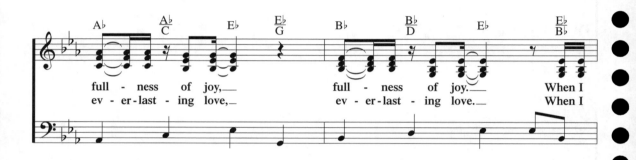

come in - to Your pres-ence, there is full - ness of joy— in the
come in - to Your pres-ence, there is ev-er-last-ing love— in the

pres - ence of the Lord, in the pres - ence of the
pres - ence of the Lord, in the pres - ence of the

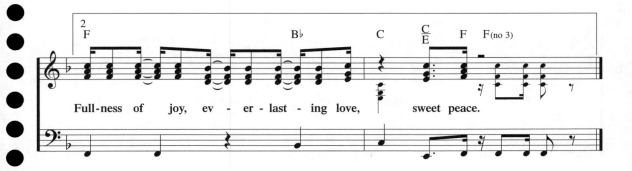

Full-ness of joy, ev-er-last-ing love, sweet peace.

Love Divine, All Loves Excelling*

1 John 4:16-17

CHARLES WESLEY

MARTY PARKS

1. Love di-vine,___ all loves ex-
2. Breathe, O breathe Thy lov-ing
3. Come, Al-might-y to De-
4. Fin-ish then___ Thy new cre-

cel - ling,
Spir - it
liv - er;
a - tion;

Joy of heav'n, to earth come___
In - to ev - 'ry trou-bled___
Let us all___ Thy life re-
Pure and spot - less let us___

81

82 Shine on Us

Psalm 80:19

M. W. S. and D. D. S.

MICHAEL W. SMITH and
DEBORAH D. SMITH

1. Lord, let Your light, light of Your face shine on us. Lord, let Your light, light of Your face shine on us. That we may be saved, that we may have
2. Lord, let Your grace, grace from Your hand fall on us. Lord, let Your grace, grace from Your hand fall on us. That we may be saved, that we may have
3. Lord, let Your love, love with no end come over us. Lord, let Your love, love with no end come over us. That we may be saved, that we may have

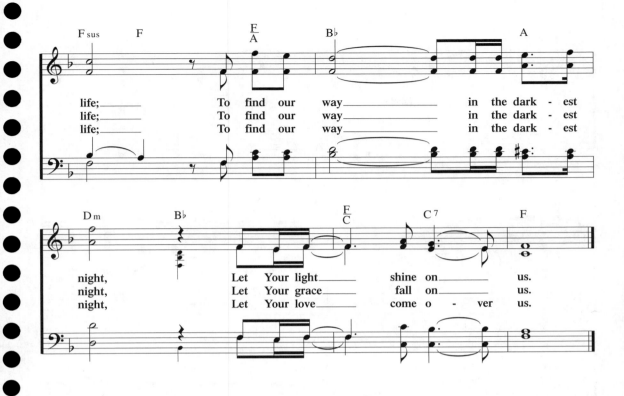

life;\
life;\
life;

To find our way in the dark - est\
To find our way in the dark - est\
To find our way in the dark - est

night,\
night,\
night,

Let Your light shine on us.\
Let Your grace fall on us.\
Let Your love come o - ver us.

My Very First Love

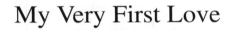

Matthew 22:37-38

83

KYLE RASMUSSEN

K. R. ♩ = ca. 84

With all my heart,___ with all my mind,___ With all my strength___

I'm going to serve___ You. Thro' ev - 'ry day,___

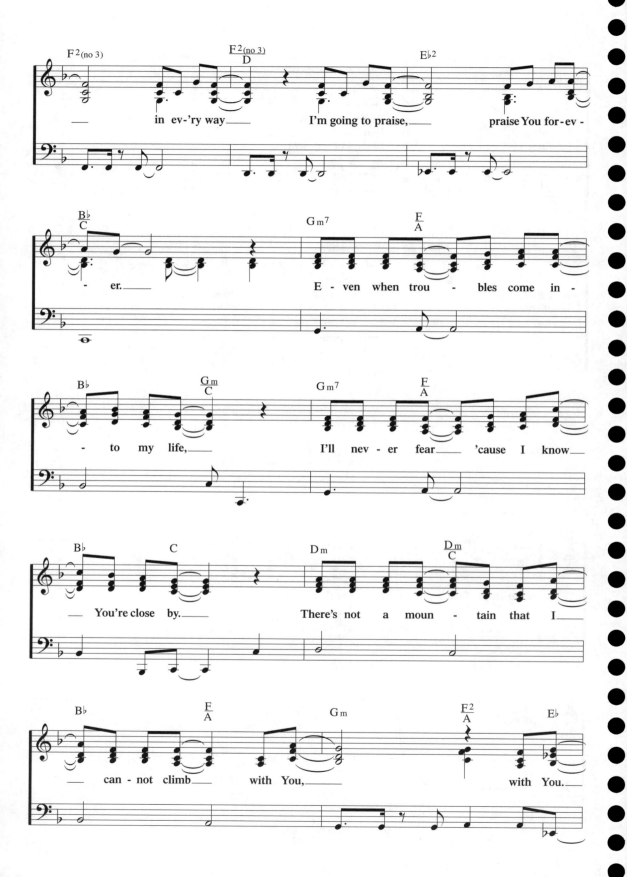

84 Jesus Christ Is the Lord of All

Philippians 2:9-11

D. W.

DAN WHITTEMORE

1. Of pres-i-dents, princ-es, rul-ers and kings,
(2. Of) heav-en's pow-ers and au-thor-i-ties,
(3. Tho') once His en-e-my in our minds,

Who of all shall reign su-preme?
On-ly He is De-i-ty.
By His blood His peace we find.

Je - sus, Je - sus, Je-sus Christ is the Lord of all.

Je - sus, Je - sus, Je-sus Christ is the Lord of

Jesus, Hail the Lamb

Revelation 5:11-14

J. H. and G. S.

JOHN HARTLEY
and GARY SADLER

1. Je - sus, hail the Lamb, with thorns Your
2. Wor - thy is the Lamb who tast - ed
3. Ho - ly is the Lamb, it was for
4. Je - sus, hail the King of sin - ners

on - ly crown; En - throned up - on the
death so cruel, Whose hands were nailed that
me You died. Com - plete sur - ren - der
rec - on - ciled. I live now ran - somed

bit - ter cross and robed with wounds for all.
formed the earth; what mer - cy for such fools.
to the cross, love's per - fect sac - ri - fice.
by Your blood, my Sav - ior, God and Friend.

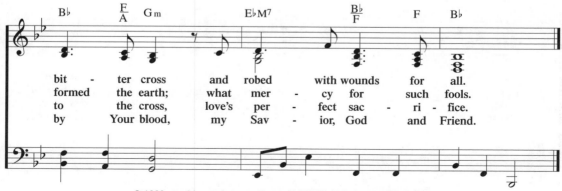

86 All People That on Earth Do Dwell

Psalm 100

WILLIAM KETHE and
Scottish Psalter, 1565

Attr. to LOUIS BOURGEOIS
Arranged by Marty Parks

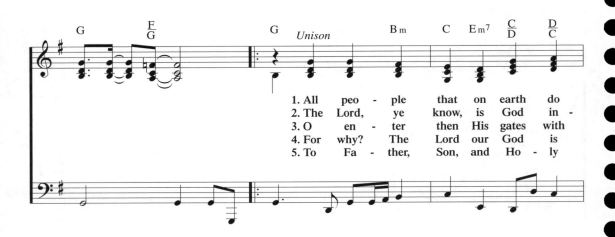

1. All peo - ple that on earth do
2. The Lord, ye know, is God in -
3. O en - ter then His gates with
4. For why? The Lord our God is
5. To Fa - ther, Son, and Ho - ly

dwell,   Sing to the
deed;   With - out our
praise;   Ap - proach with
good;   His mer - cy
Ghost,   The God whom

87 Holy Lamb of God

Revelation 5:11-13

M. L.

MOSIE LISTER

1. In this ho - ly place we bow to - day and
2. Ho - ly Prince of Peace, Em - man - u - el, Be -

wor - ship the King of Heav - en. In this place, from all the
got - ten of the Fa - ther, Come to - day with - in our

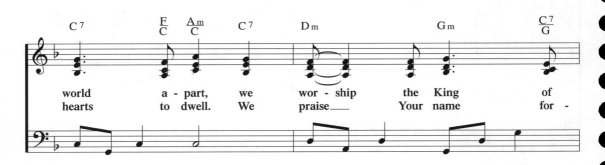

world a - part, we wor - ship the King of
hearts to dwell. We praise Your name for -

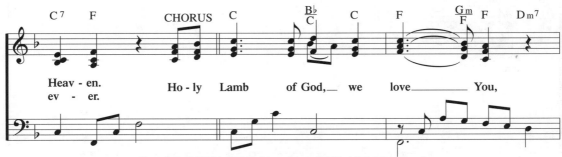

Heav - en.
ev - er.

CHORUS Ho - ly Lamb of God, we love You,

love_____ You,_____ love_____ You. You are Lord of ev - 'ry -
thing we are. Ho - ly Lamb of God, we love You.

Father, I Adore You

88

Matthew 22:37-38

T. C. S.

TERRYE COELHO STROM

1. Fa - ther, I a - dore You, Lay my life be -
2. Je - sus, I a - dore You, Lay my life be -
3. Spir - it, I a - dore You, Lay my life be -

fore You. How I love_____ You!
fore You. How I love_____ You!
fore You. How I love_____ You!

89 Every Generation*

Psalm 45:17; Philippians 2:9-11

BRUCE WICKERSHEIM

We Sing Worthy

Revelation 5:11-14

91

Amazing

Matthew 10:8; Romans 5:17, 20

M. R.   ♩ = ca. 136

MATT REDMAN

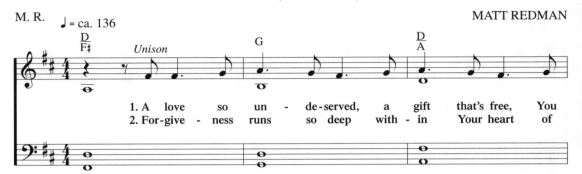

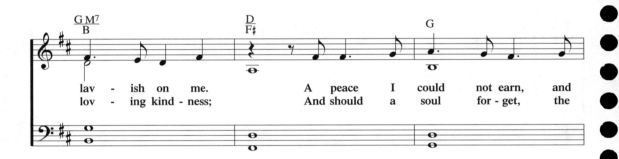

1. A love so un - de-served, a gift that's free, You
2. For-give - ness runs so deep with - in Your heart of

lav - ish on me.   A peace I could not earn, and
lov - ing kind - ness;   And should a soul for - get, the

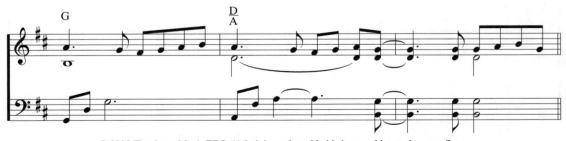

mer - cy for the free - dom of my soul.
cross of Christ re - minds us ev - 'ry day.

give my life to You._____ And

I Remember You*

92

1 Corinthians 11:23-26

C. H.

CHRISTINE HAYS

I take this_____ bread, bro - ken for

me, And I thank You, Lord,_____ for all You've

done._____ I take this_____

93 Let It Be Said of Us

Galatians 6:14; 2 Timothy 4:7-8

STEVE FRY

1. Let it be said of us, that the Lord was our pas- sion, That with glad- ness we bore ev- 'ry cross we were giv- en, That we fought the good fight, that we fin- ished the course, Know- ing with- in us the pow'r of the ris- en Lord.

2. Let it be said of us, we were marked by for- give- ness, We were known by our love, and de- light- ed in meek- ness. We were ruled by His peace, heed- ing u- ni- ty's call, Joined as one bod- y that Christ would be seen by all.

Let the

94

Draw Us with Your Love*

Psalm 100:4

SUSAN SACCA

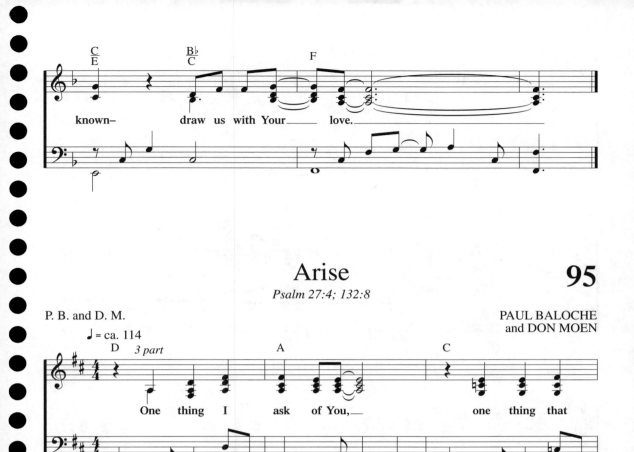

Arise

Psalm 27:4; 132:8

95

P. B. and D. M.

PAUL BALOCHE
and DON MOEN

♩ = ca. 114

3 part

One thing I ask of You,— one thing that

we de-sire;— That as we wor-ship You,—

Lord, come and change our— lives.— A-rise,

96

Majesty (Here I Am)

Isaiah 6:1-8

M. S. and S. G.

MARTIN SMITH and
STUART GARRARD

1. Here I am, hum-bled by Your maj - es - ty,
2. Here I am, hum-bled by the love that You give,

Cov-ered by Your grace so free.
For - giv - en so that I can for - give.

Here I am, know-ing I'm a sin - ful man,
Here I stand, know-ing that I'm Your de - sire,

Cov - ered by the blood of the Lamb.
Sanc - ti - fied by glo - ry and fire.

Sing-ing, Maj - es - ty,_____

Maj - es - ty,_____ For - ev - er I am changed by Your love,_____

In the pres - ence of Your Maj - es - ty,_____

Maj - es - ty._____

 97

Holy, Holy

Revelation 4:8

MARY MACLEAN

M. M.

Ho - ly, ho - ly! Lord, God Al - might - y, Who was and

98

Doxology

Psalm 150:6

THOMAS KEN

MARTY PARKS

Praise God from whom all bless-ings flow. Praise Him, all crea-tures here be - low. Praise Him a - bove, ye heav'n-ly host. Praise Fa - ther, Son, and Ho - ly Ghost.

I Love You, Lord

Psalm 18:1

99

L. K.

LAURIE KLEIN

I love You, Lord, and I lift my voice
To worship You; O my soul, re - joice!
Take joy, my King, in what You hear;
May it be a sweet, sweet sound in Your ear.

100

God of Grace

Romans 5:17, 20

K. G. and J. R.

KEITH GETTY and
JONATHAN REA

1. God of Grace, a - maz - ing won - der, strong and mea - sure - less and free. O the mir - a - cle of mer - cy, Je - sus reach - es down to me. God of Grace, I stand and won - der as my God re - stores my
2. God of Grace, who loved and knew me long be - fore the world be - gan, Sent my Sav - ior down from heav - en, Per - fect God and per - fect man. God of Grace, I trust in Je - sus, I'm ac - cept - ed as His
3. God of Grace, I stand as - tound - ed, cleansed, for - giv - en and se - cure. All my fears are now con - found - ed and my hope is ev - er sure. God of Grace, now crowned in glo - ry where one day I'll see Your

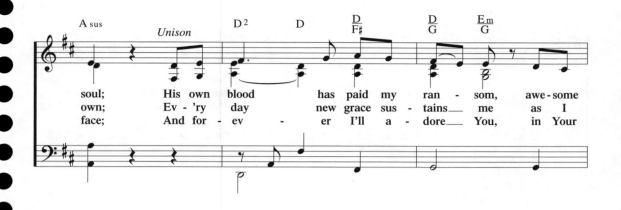

soul; His own blood has paid my ran - som, awe - some
own; Ev - 'ry day new grace sus - tains___ me as I
face; And for - ev - er I'll a - dore___ You, in Your

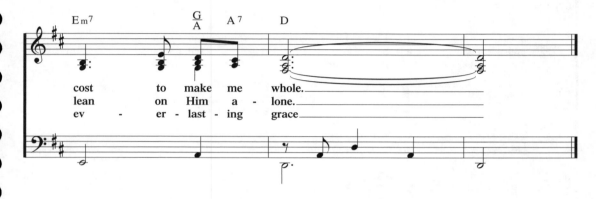

cost to make me whole.___
lean on Him a - lone.___
ev - er - last - ing grace___

Jesus, Draw Me Ever Nearer

101

Psalm 17:7-8, 15

M. B. and K. G.

MARGARET BECKER
and KEITH GETTY

♩ = ca. 68

1. Je - sus,___ draw me ev - er near - er as I
(2. Je - sus,)___ guide me through the tem - pest, keep my
(3. Let the)___ trea - sures of the tri - al form with -

Dwell in Me

Colossians 3:16

102

M. P.

MARTY PARKS

103

A Shield About Me

Psalm 3:3

D. T. and C. W.

DONN THOMAS and
CHARLES WILLIAMS

Thou, O Lord, are a shield a-bout me. You're my glo-ry; You're the lift-er of my head. head. Hal-le-lu-jah, hal-le-lu-jah, hal-le-lu-jah, You're the

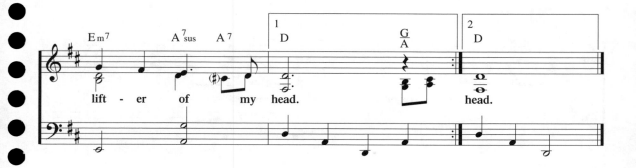

Be Glorified

Philippians 1:20

104

L. G. and C. T.

LOUIE GIGLIO and
CHRIS TOMLIN

Your love— has cap-tured me,— Your grace— has set me— free;— Your life,— the air— I— breathe.

Be glo-ri-fied— in me.

105

O How I Love Jesus

1 Peter 1:8

FREDERICK WHITFIELD

Traditional American Melody
Arranged by Marty Parks

1. There is a name I love to hear; I love to sing its worth. It sounds like mu - sic in my ear, The sweet - est name on earth.

(2. It) tells me of a Sav - ior's love, Who died to set me free. It tells me of His pre - cious blood, The sin - ner's per - fect plea.

(3. It) tells of One whose lov - ing heart Can feel my deep - est woe, Who in each sor - row bears a part That none can bear be - low.

106

Lord, from Your Hand

Luke 22:15-20; 23:33-49

KEN BIBLE

English Folk Melody

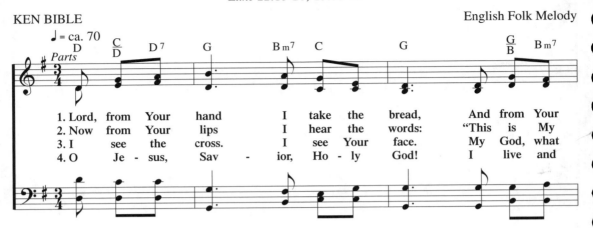

1. Lord, from Your hand I take the bread, And from Your
2. Now from Your hand lips I hear the words: "This is My
3. I see the cross. I see Your face. My God, what
4. O Je - sus, Sav - ior, Ho - ly God! I live and

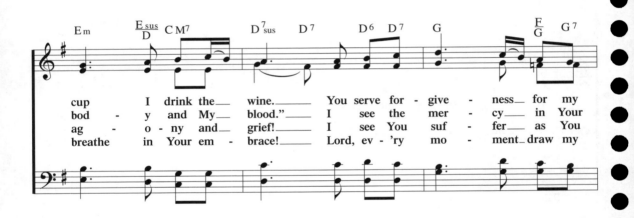

cup I drink the wine. You serve for - give - ness for my
bod - y and My blood." I see the mer - cy in Your
ag - o - ny and grief! I see You suf - fer as You
breathe in Your em - brace! Lord, ev - 'ry mo - ment draw my

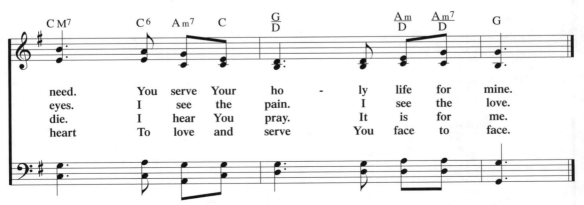

need. You serve Your ho - ly life for mine.
eyes. I see the pain. I see the love.
die. I hear You pray. It is for me.
heart To love and serve You face to face.

Healing Rain

Hosea 6:1-3

107

M. W. S., M. S. and M. B.

MICHAEL W. SMITH,
MARTIN SMITH
and MATT BRONLEEWE

♩ = ca. 72
Unison

1. Heal - ing rain_____ is com - ing down,_____ It's com-ing
(2. Heal - ing rain)_____ is com - ing down,_____ It's com-ing
(3. Lift your heads:)_____ let us re-turn_____ To the

near - er_____ to_____ this old town;_____ The rich and poor,_____
clos - er_____ to the lost and found._____ Tears of joy_____
mer - cy seat,_____ where time be - gan;_____ And in your eyes_____

the weak and_____ strong, It's bring - ing
and tears of_____ shame, A - wash for-
I see the_____ pain, Come salve this

mer - cy;_____ it won't be long.
- ev - er_____ in Je - sus' name.
dry heart_____ with heal - ing rain.

108 All the Nations

Revelation 5:9-10

C. D.

CHRIS DAVIS

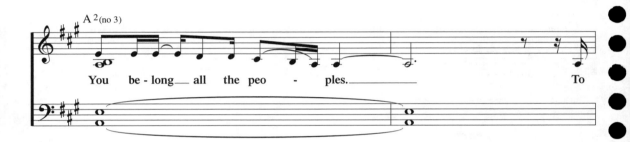

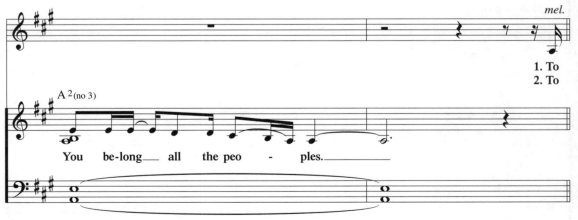

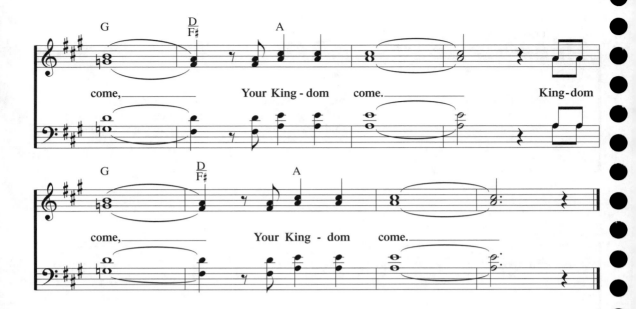

109

I Will Bow to You

Psalm 95:6

P. E.   ♩ = ca. 62

PETE EPISCOPO

Lord, I will bow___ to You, to no oth - er god___

but You___ a - lone.

Lord, I will wor - ship You, noth-ing hands___ have made

110 Eagles Wings

Isaiah 40:31

R. M.

REUBEN MORGAN

Here I am wait - ing,_____ a - bide in me,___ I pray.___

Here I am long - ing_____ for You.___

Hide me in Your___ love,___

bring me to___ my knees;___ May I know Je -

- sus more and more.___

Come, live in me, all my life take o-ver; Come, breathe in me, I will rise on ea-gle's wings.

Come, Let Us Worship and Bow Down 111
Psalm 96:6-7

Adapted by D. D.

DAVE DOHERTY

♩ = ca. 80

Unison

Come, let us wor-ship and bow down; Let us

hand,   just the sheep_____ of His hand.

All Heaven Declares

Psalm 19:1; Revelation 5:13-14

N. R. and T. R.

NOEL RICHARDS and
TRICIA RICHARDS

1. All heav'n de-clares   the glo-ry of__ the
2. I will pro-claim   the glo-ry of__ the

ris - en Lord.   Who can   com - pare
ris - en Lord.   Who once   was slain

112

Come Now Before Him

Psalm 100:4

113

G. B.

GAYLEN BOURLAND

114 Before the Throne of God Above

Hebrews 4:14; 7:25

CHARITIE L. BANCROFT
and VIKKI COOK

VIKKI COOK

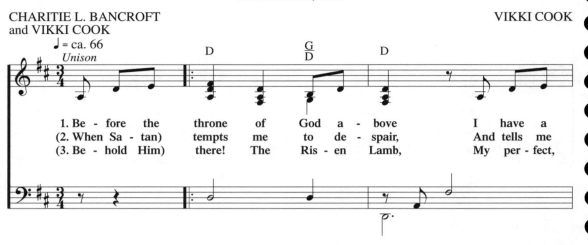

1. Be - fore the throne of God a - bove, I have a
(2. When Sa - tan) tempts me to de - spair, And tells me
(3. Be - hold Him) there! The Ris - en Lamb, My per - fect,

strong and per - fect plea; A great High Priest whose name is
of the guilt with - in. Up - ward I look and see Him
spot - less Righ - teous - ness; The great un - change - a - ble I

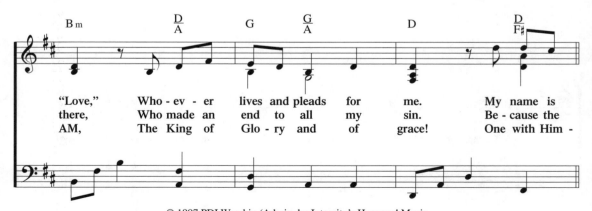

"Love," Who - ev - er lives and pleads for me. My name is
there, Who made an end to all my sin. Be - cause the
AM, The King of Glo - ry and of grace! The One with Him -

115 Blessing, Honor and Glory

Revelation 5:13

G. B. and D. R.

GEOFF BULLOCK
and DAVID REIDY

Lamb of God! He is the Lamb of God! He is the Lamb of God!

Bless the Lord, O My Soul

Psalm 103:1

116

Adapted

Unknown

Bless the Lord, O my soul; Bless the Lord, O my soul;

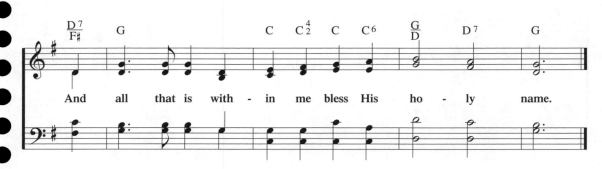

And all that is with-in me bless His ho-ly name.

117

By the Blood

Hebrews 9:11-14

C. and D. M.

CHRIS and DIANE MACHEN

By the blood of an in-no-cent One;

By the blood, by the blood,

By the blood of Je-sus, Your Son.

Show Me Your Ways

118

Psalm 25:4-5

R. F.

RUSSELL FRAGAR

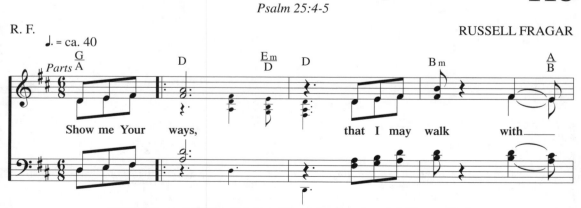

Show me Your ways, that I may walk with

Send It on Down

Joel 2:28-29; Acts 1:8

119

G. D.

GERON DAVIS

Send it on down, send it on down.

Lord, let the Ho-ly Ghost come on down.

Send it on down, send it on down.

Lord, let the Ho-ly Ghost come on down.

Lord, we're Your chil-dren, and we are ask-ing

120

I Will Sing

Psalm 108:1-5

C. C.

CHRISTY COOPER

Lyrics:
I will sing____ of Your glo - ry, Your ex - cel-lent works, I will sing____
of Your pow - er thro' - out____ all the earth; I will sing____
of Your joy,____ Your im - meas - ur - 'ble worth. I will sing____
of my Lord____ and my King.____ I will sing____
2. I will sing, I will sing;____
I will sing,

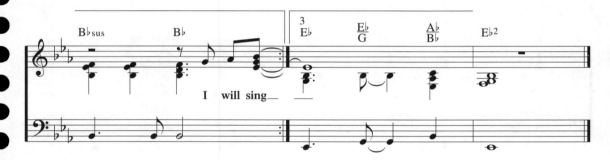

Good to Me

Psalm 142

121

C. M.

CRAIG MUSSEAU

I_____ cry out for Your hand of mer-cy to

122 Holy Is the Lord

Isaiah 6:3; John 1:14

KEN BIBLE and Traditional

FRANZ SCHUBERT

Ho - ly, ho - ly, ho - ly, Ho - ly is the Lord.___

Ho - ly, ho - ly, ho - ly, Ho - ly is the Lord.___

Word of God the Fa - ther, Full of truth and grace,___

Life and Light of heav - en, We have seen Your face.

I Walk by Faith

2 Corinthians 5:7

CHRIS FALSON

123

124 Lion of Judah

Revelation 5:11-14; 19:16

R. M.

ROBIN MARK

1. You're the Li - on of Ju - dah, the Lamb___ Who was slain, You as-
2. There's a shield in our hand and a sword___ at our side, There's a

cend - ed to Heav - en and ev - er-more will reign. At the
fire in our spir - its that can-not be de - nied; 'Cause the

end of the age___ when the earth You re - claim,___ You will
Fa - ther has told us, for___ these You have died,___ For the

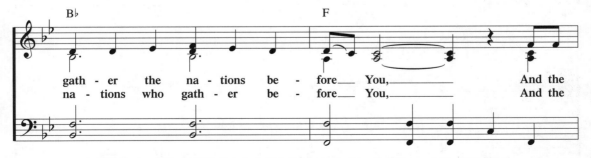

gath - er the na - tions be - fore___ You,___ And the
na - tions who gath - er be - fore___ You,___ And the

125 I Want to Know Him

Philippians 3:10

D. W. ♩ = ca. 63

DAN WHITTEMORE

O__ I, I want to know Him and the pow-er of His res-ur-

126 Holy Is the Lord

Revelation 4:8

C. C.

CHRISTY COOPER

127 Give Us Clean Hands

Psalm 24:3-6

C. H.

CHARLIE HALL

Give us clean hands,____ give us pure hearts;____

Let us not lift our souls____ to an-

oth-er. Give us clean hands,____ give us pure hearts;____

Let us not lift our souls____ to an-

128 Under Your Wing

Psalm 91:4; 121

C. C.

CHRISTY COOPER

O Mighty Cross

1 Corinthians 1:18

129

130 No Other Gods

Exodus 20:2-3

D. M.

DAVID MOFFITT

1. The God of__ the heav - ens, (The God of__ the heav - ens,) the
2. Our Mak - er,__ Cre - a - tor (Our Mak - er,__ Cre - a - tor) be -

An - cient__ of Days, (the An - cient__ of Days,) The
fore time__ be - gan, (be - fore time__ be - gan,) Mes -

God of__ our Fa - thers (The God of__ our Fa - thers) and
si - ah__ and Sav - ior, (Mes - si - ah__ and Sav - ior,) Re -

God of__ my__ praise, (and God of__ my__ praise,) The
deem - er__ and__ Friend, (Re - deem - er__ and__ Friend,) Our

131 Only a God like You

1 Chronicles 29:10-13

T. W.

TOMMY WALKER

For the prais - es— of man,— I will

nev - er, ev - er stand.————— For the

king - doms of—— this world,—— I'll nev - er give—

— my heart a - way or shout—— my praise.—— My al -

132 White as Snow

Isaiah 1:18

L. O. ♩ = ca. 92

LEON OLGUIN

White as snow, white as snow, Though my
sins were as scar - let, Lord, I know. Lord, I know
that I'm clean and for - giv - en. Thro' the
pow - er of Your blood, Thro' the won - der of Your love,
Thro' faith in You I know That I can

Christ in Us Be Glorified

Philippians 1:20

134 Consuming Fire

Acts 1:8

T. H.

TIM HUGHES

3 part ♩ = ca. 76

1. There must be more_____ than this; O breath of God_____
2. Come like a rush_____ing wind, Clothe us in pow-

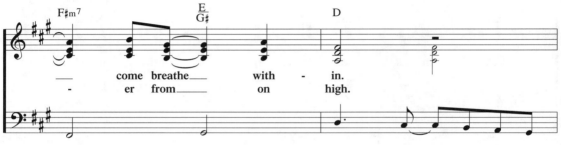

_____ come breathe_____ with in.
- er from_____ on high.

There must be more_____ than this; Spir - it of God_____
Now set the cap - tives free; Leave us a - ban -

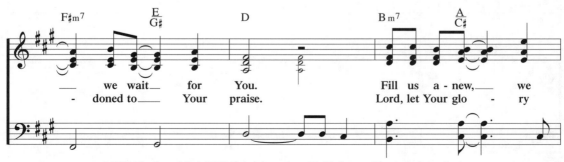

_____ we wait_____ for You. Fill us a - new,_____ we
- doned to_____ Your praise. Lord, let Your glo - ry

135
When I Think About the Lord
Psalm 40:1-3

J. H.

JAMES HUEY

Lyrics:

When I think a-bout the Lord, how He saved me, how He raised me, How He filled me with the Ho-ly Ghost, how He healed me to the ut-ter-most; When I think a-bout the Lord, how He picked me up and turned me a-round, How He placed my feet on sol-id ground. It

136 Holy Spirit, Rain Down

Hosea 6:1-3; 1 Corinthians 2:9-10

RUSSELL FRAGAR

Made Me Glad

137

Psalm 34:1-4; 40:1-3; 73:25; 91:2-6

M. W.

MIRIAM WEBSTER

I will bless the Lord for-ev - er.

I will trust Him at all times.

He has de-

liv - ered me from all fear.

138 You Are Good

Psalm 136:1

ISRAEL HOUGHTON

I. H.

♩ = ca. 120

Lord, You_ are good and_ Your mer - cy_ en - dur - eth_ for - ev - er._

Lord, You_ are good and_ Your mer - cy_ en - dur - eth_ for - ev - er._

Peo - ple_ from ev - er - y

139   I Will Never Be (the Same Again)

Philippians 3:12-14

GEOFF BULLOCK

1. I will nev-er be_____ the same_ a-gain;
I can nev-er re-turn,_ I've closed the door._

140 Yesterday, Today and Forever

Hebrews 13:8

V. B.

VICKY BEECHING

1. Ev - er - last-ing God,_____ the years go by, but You're
2. Un - cre - a - ted One,_____ You have no end and no_____

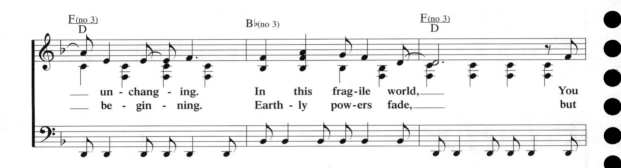

_____ un - chang - ing. In this frag-ile world,_____ You
_____ be - gin - ning. Earth - ly pow-ers fade,_____ but

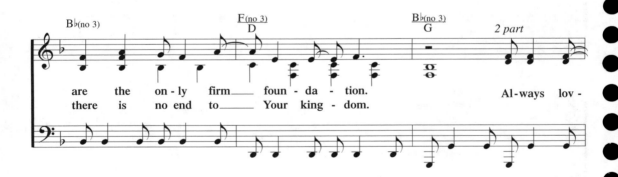

are the on - ly firm_____ foun - da - tion.
there is no end to_____ Your king - dom.

Al - ways lov -

- ing, al - ways_____ true,

Everyday

Psalm 146:2

141

J. H. ♩ = ca. 120

JOEL HOUSTON

1. What to say, Lord? It's You who gave me life and I can't ex-plain just how much You mean to me now

Lord Most High

Psalm 22:22-31

142

D. H. and G. S.

DON HARRIS and
GARY SADLER

From the ends of the earth, From the depths of the sea; From the heights of the heav-ens Your name be praised; From the hearts of the weak, From the shouts of the strong;

INDEX OF SCRIPTURE BACKGROUNDS

*Songs marked with an asterisk (*) are included on the companion recordings.

INDEX OF KEYS AND METER SIGNATURES

*Songs marked with an asterisk (*) are included on the companion recordings.

TOPICAL INDEX WITH KEYS

*Songs marked with an asterisk (*) are included on the companion recordings.

ALPHABETICAL INDEX WITH KEYS

*Songs marked with an asterisk (*) are included on the companion recordings.